Poems by John B Tabb

London John Lane
Boston Copeland and Day
MDCCCXCIV

University Press:
John Wilson and Son, Cambridge, U.S.A.

AVE: SIDNEY LANIER.

ERE Time's horizon-line was set,
Somewhere in space our spirits met,
Then o'er the starry parapet
Came wandering here.
And now, that thou art gone again
Beyond the verge, I haste amain
(Lost echo of a loftier strain)
To greet thee there.

CONTENTS.

QUATRAINS.

SONNETS.

THE RING.

HOLD the trinket near thine eye,
And it circles earth and sky;
Place it further, and behold!
But a finger's breadth of gold.

Thus our lives, beloved, lie
Ringed with love's fair boundary;
Place it further, and its sphere
Measures but a falling tear.

LIMITATION.

BREATHE above me or below;
Never canst thou farther go
Than the spirit's octave-span,
Harmonizing God and Man.

Thus within the iris-bound,
Light a prisoner is found;
Thus within my soul I see
Life in Time's captivity.

NEKROS.

LO! all thy glory gone!
God's masterpiece undone!
The last created and the first to fall;
The noblest, frailest, godliest of all.

Death seems the conqueror now,
And yet his victor thou:
The fatal shaft, its venom quench'd in thee,
A mortal raised to immortality.

Child of the humble sod,
Wed with the breath of God,
Descend! for with the lowest thou must lie —
Arise! thou hast inherited the sky.

WESTWARD.

AND dost thou lead him hence with thee,
  O setting sun,
And leave the shadows all to me
  When he is gone?
Ah, if my grief his guerdon be,
  My dark his light,
I count each loss felicity,
  And bless the night.

TO A PHOTOGRAPH.

O TENDER shade!
  Lone captive of enamoured Light,
That from an angel visage bright
  A glance betrayed.

  Dost thou not sigh
To wander from thy prison-place?
To seek again the vanished face,
  Or else, to die?

  A shade like thee,
Dim Eidolon — a dream disproved —
A memory of light removed,
  Behold in me!

MY STAR.

SINCE that the dewdrop holds the star
  The long night through,
Perchance the satellite afar
  Reflects the dew.

And while thine image in my heart
  Doth steadfast shine;
There, haply, in thy heaven apart
  Thou keepest mine.

CONTENT.

WERE all the heavens an overladen bough
  Of ripened benediction lowered above me,
What could I crave, soul-satisfied as now
  That thou dost love me?

The door is shut. To each unsheltered Blessing
  Henceforth I say, "Depart! What would'st thou
      of me?"
Beggared I am of want, this boon possessing,
  That thou dost love me.

ROBIN.

COME to me, Robin! The daylight is dying!
  Come to me now!
Come, ere the cypress-tree over me sighing,
Dank with the shadow-tide, circle my brow;
Come, ere oblivion speed to me, flying
  Swifter than thou!

Come to me, Robin! The far echoes waken
  Cold to my cry!
Oh! with the swallow-wing, love overtaken,
Hence to the Echo-land, homeward, to fly!
Thou art my life, Robin. Oh! love-forsaken,
  How can I die?

THE WHITE JESSAMINE.

I KNEW she lay above me,
  Where the casement all the night
Shone, softened with a phosphor glow
  Of sympathetic light,
And that her fledgling spirit pure
  Was pluming fast for flight.

Each tendril throbbed and quickened
  As I nightly climbed apace,
And could scarce restrain the blossoms
  When, anear the destined place,
Her gentle whisper thrilled me
  Ere I gazed upon her face.

I waited, darkling, till the dawn
  Should touch me into bloom,
While all my being panted
  To outpour its first perfume,
When, lo! a paler flower than mine
  Had blossomed in the gloom!

THE CLOUD.

FAR on the brink of day
Thou standest as the herald of the dawn,
Where fades the night's last flickering spark away
Ere the first dewdrop 's gone.

Above the eternal snows
By winter scattered on the mountain height
To shroud the centuries, thy visage glows
With a prophetic light.

Calm is thine awful brow;
As when thy presence shrined Divinity
Between the flaming Cherubim, so now
Its shadow clings to thee.

Yet as an Angel mild
Thou, in the torrid noon, with sheltering wing
Dost o'er the earth, as to a weary child,
A balm celestial bring.

And when the evening dies,
Still to thy fringed vesture cleaves the light —
The last sad glimmer of her tearful eyes
On the dark verge of night.

So, soon thy glories wane!
Thou too must mourn the rose of morning shed:
Cold creeps the fatal shadow o'er thy train,
And settles on thy head.

And while the wistful eye
Yearns for the charm that wooed its ravished gaze,
The sympathy of Nature wakes a sigh,
And thus its thought betrays:

"Thou, like the Cloud, my soul,
Dost in thyself of beauty nought possess;
Devoid the light of Heaven, a vapor foul,
The veil of nothingness!"

PHANTOMS.

ARE ye the ghosts of fallen leaves,
  O flakes of snow,
For which, through naked trees, the winds
  A-mourning go?

Or are ye angels, bearing home
  The host unseen
Of truant spirits, to be clad
  Again in green?

THE VOYAGERS.

THE Spring in festival array,
  From Death to Life, from Night to Day,
    Came floating o'er the main;
And now with banners brave and bright,
From Life to Death, from Day to Night,
    The Autumn drifts again.

THE SWALLOW.

SKIM o'er the tide,
And from thy pinions fling
The sparkling water-drops,
Sweet child of spring!
Bathe in the dying sunshine warm and bright,
Till ebbs the last receding wave of light.

Swift glides the hour,
But what its flight to thee?
Thine own is fleeter far;
E'en now to me
Thou seem'st upon futurity anon
To beckon thence the tardy present on.

The eye in vain
Pursues, with subtle glance,
Thy dim, delirious course
Through heaven's expanse:
Vanished thy form upon the wings of thought,
Ere yet its place the lagging vision caught.

Again thou'rt here,
A slanting arrow sent
From yon fair-tinted bow,
In promise bent;
As when, erewhile, the gentle bird of love
Poised her white wing the new-born land above.

A seeming shade,
Scarce palpable in form,
Yet thine, alas, the change
Of calm and storm!
The veering passions of my stronger soul
Alike the throbbings of thy heart control.

For day is done,
And cloyed of long delight,
Like me thou welcomest
The sober night;
Like me, aweary, sinkest on that breast,
That woos all nature to her silent rest.

CLOISTERED.

WITHIN the compass of mine eyes
Behold, a lordly city lies —
  A world to me unknown,
Save that along its crowded ways
Moves one whose heart in other days
  Was mated to mine own.

I ask no more; enough for me
One heaven above us both to see,
  One calm horizon-line
Around us, like a mystic ring
That Love has set, encompassing
  That kindred life and mine.

THE LONELY MOUNTAIN.

ONE bird, that ever with the wakening spring
  Was wont to sing,
I wait, through all my woodlands, far and near,
  In vain to hear.

The voice of many waters, silent long
  Breaks forth in song;
Young breezes to the listening leaves outpour
  Their heavenly lore:

A thousand other wingèd warblers sweet,
  Returning, greet
Their fellows, and rebuild upon my breast
  The wonted nest.

But unto me one fond familiar strain
  Comes not again —
A breath whose faintest echo, farthest heard,
  A mountain stirred.

ECHOES.

WHERE of old, responsive
As the wind and foam,
Rose the joyous echoes,
Desolate I roam,
Nor find one lingering sound to hail the wanderer home.

Silence, long unbroken,
Break thy rigid spell!
Free the fairy captives
Of the mountain dell,
If yet in veiling mist the mimic minions dwell.

Children of the distance,
Shall I call in vain?
From your slumbers waking,
Speak to me again
As erst in childhood woke your soft Æolian strain!

Hark! the wavy chorus,
Faint and far away,
Like a dream returning
In the light of day, —
Too fond to flee; alas! too timorous to stay!

Hints of heavenly voices,
Tone for silvery tone,
Move in rarer measures

Than to us are known,
Still wooing hence to worlds beyond the shadowy zone.

Pausing, still they linger
As in love's delay,
With sibyllic omen
Seeming thus to say;
"Of all the vanished Past, we Echoes only stay!"

PHOTOGRAPHED.

FOR years, an ever-shifting shade
The sunshine of thy visage made;
Then, spider-like, the captive caught
In meshes of immortal thought.

E'en so, with half-averted eye,
Day after day I passed thee by,
Till suddenly, a subtler art
Enshrined thee in my heart of heart.

THE HALF-RING MOON.

OVER the sea, over the sea,
My love he is gone to a far countrie;
But he brake a golden ring with me
The pledge of his faith to be.

Over the sea, over the sea,
He comes no more from the far countrie;
But at night, where the new moon loved to be,
Hangs the half of a ring for me.

ENSHRINED.

COME quickly in and close the door,
For none hath entered here before,
The secret chamber set apart
Within the cloister of the heart.

Tread softly! 'T is the Holy Place
Where memory meets face to face
A sacred sorrow, felt of yore,
But sleeping now forevermore.

It cannot die; for nought of pain,
Its fleeting vesture, doth remain:
Behold upon the shrouded eye
The seal of immortality!

Love would not wake it, nor efface
Of anguish one abiding trace,
Since e'en the calm of heaven were less,
Untouched of human tenderness.

IN MY ORANGE-GROVE

ORBS of Autumnal beauty, breathed to light
From blooms of May,
Rounded between the touch of lengthening night
And lessening day,
Flushed with the Summer fulness that the Spring
(Fair seer!) foretold,
The circle of three seasons compassing
In spheres of gold.

INTIMATIONS.

I KNEW the flowers had dreamed of you,
And hailed the morning with regret;
For all their faces with the dew
Of vanished joy were wet.

I knew the winds had passed your way,
Though not a sound the truth betrayed;
About their pinions all the day
A summer fragrance stayed.

And so, awaking or asleep,
A memory of lost delight
By day the sightless breezes keep,
And silent flowers by night.

EVOLUTION.

OUT of the dusk a shadow,
  Then, a spark;
Out of the cloud a silence,
  Then, a lark;
Out of the heart a rapture,
  Then, a pain;
Out of the dead, cold ashes,
  Life again.

LOVE'S HYBLA.

MY thoughts fly to thee, as the bees
  To find their favorite flower;
Then home, with honeyed memories
  Of many a fragrant hour:

For with thee is the place apart
  Where sunshine ever dwells,
The Hybla, whence my hoarding heart
  Would fill its wintry cells.

WAYFARERS.

O COMRADE Sun, that day by day
Dost weave a shadow on my way,
Lest, in the luxury of light,
My soul forget the neighboring night: —
Wilt thou whene'er, my journey done,
Thou wanderest our path upon,
Bear in thy beams a memory
Of one who walked the world with thee,
Or mourn, amid the lavishness
Of Life, one hovering shade the less?

THE PEAK.

AS on some solitary height
Abides, in summer's fierce despite,
Snow-blossom that no sun can blight,
  No frost can kill;
So, in my soul, — all else below
To change succumbing, — stands aglow
One wreath of immemorial snow,
  Unscattered still.

THE CAPTIVES.

APART forever dwelt the twain,
Save for one oft-repeated strain
Wherein what Love alone could say
They learned and lavished day by day.

Strangers in all but misery
And music's hope-sustaining tie,
They lived and loved and died apart,
But soul to soul and heart to heart.

MY PHOTOGRAPH.

MY sister Sunshine smiled on me,
And of my visage wrought a shade.
"Behold," she cried, "the mystery
Of which thou art afraid!

"For Death is but a tenderness,
A shadow, that unclouded Love
Hath fashioned in its own excess
Of radiance from above."

BROTHERHOOD.

KNEW not the Sun, sweet Violet,
  The while he gleaned the snow,
That thou in darkness sepulchred,
  Wast slumbering below?
Or spun a splendor of surprise
Around him to behold thee rise?

Saw not the Star, sweet Violet,
  What time a drop of dew
Let fall his image from the sky
  Into thy deeper blue?
Nor waxed he tremulous and dim
When rival Dawn supplanted him?

And dreamest thou, sweet Violet,
  That I, the vanished Star,
The Dewdrop, and the morning Sun,
  Thy closest kinsmen are —
So near that, waking or asleep,
We each and all thine image keep?

EVICTED.

TIME shut the door, and turned the key;
And here in darkness (woe is me!)
  I wait and call in vain:
  He will not come again!
I had but stepped beyond the light,
And on the threshold of the night
  Turned back — alas, to find
  Life's portal closed behind!

Breathless, I beat the ponderous door:
No answer! Silence evermore,
  Remembering what has been,
  Sits desolate within.
The Present dead, Futurity,
Its still-born babe, wakes not for me:
  I am alone at last
  With the immortal Past.

GRIEF–SONG.

NEW grief, new tears; —
  Brief the reign of sorrow;
Clouds that gather with the night
  Scatter on the morrow.

Old grief, old tears; —
  Come and gone together;
Not a fleck upon the sky
  Telling whence or whither.

Old grief, new tears ; —
  Deep to deep is calling:
Life is but a passing cloud
  Whence the rain is falling.

RECOGNITION.

AT twilight, on the open sea,
We passed, with breath of melody—
A song, to each familiar, sung
In accents of an alien tongue.

We could not see each other's face,
Nor through the growing darkness trace
Our destinies; but brimming eyes
Betrayed unworded sympathies.

AN INFLUENCE.

I SEE thee,— heaven's unclouded face
  A vacancy around thee made,
Its sunshine a subservient grace
  Thy lovelier light to shade.

I feel thee, as the billows feel
  A river freshening the brine;
A life's libation poured to heal
  The bitterness of mine.

HELPMATES.

SAYS the Land, "O sister Sea,
Had'st thou not borne the voyagers to me,
Vain were their visions grand,
And I, e'en now, perchance, a stranger-land:
  So, thine the glory be!"

Says the Sea, "Nay, brother Land;
Had'st thou not outward stretched the saving hand,
My bosom now had kept
The secret where the souls heroic slept;
  'Tis in thy strength they stand!"

TO MY SHADOW.

FRIEND forever in the light
   Cleaving to my side,
Harbinger of endless night
   That must soon betide;

"Hither," seemest thou to say,
   "From the twilight now:
In the darkness when I stay,
   Never thence wilt thou."

THE LAKE.

I AM a lonely woodland lake:
  The trees that round me grow,
The glimpse of heaven above me, make
  The sum of all I know.

The mirror of their dreams to be
  Alike in shade and shine,
To clasp in Love's captivity,
  And keep them one — is mine.

THE DAYSPRING.

WHAT hand with spear of light
Hath cleft the side of Night,
And from the red wound wide
Fashioned the Dawn, his bride?

Was it the deed of Death?
Nay; but of Love, that saith,
"Henceforth be Shade and Sun,
In bonds of Beauty, one."

THE CHORD.

IN this narrow cloister bound
Dwells a Sisterhood of Sound,
Far from alien voices rude
As in secret solitude
Unisons, that yearned apart,
Here, in harmony of heart,
Blend divided sympathies,
And in choral strength arise,
Like the cloven tongues of fire,
One in heavenly desire.

COMPENSATION.

HOW many an acorn falls to die
  For one that makes a tree!
How many a heart must pass me by
  For one that cleaves to me!

How many a suppliant wave of sound
  Must still unheeded roll,
For one low utterance that found
  An echo in my soul!

VISIBLE SOUND.

AYE, have we not felt it and known,
Ere Science proclaimed it her own,
That form is but visible tone?

Behold, where in silence was drowned
The last fleeting echo of sound,
The rainbow — its blossom — is found;

While anon, with a verdurous sweep
From the mountain-side, wooded and steep,
Swells the chorus of deep unto deep,

That the trumpet flowers, flame-flashing, blow
Till the lilies enkindled below
Swoon pale into passion, like snow!

Yea, Love, of sweet Nature the Lord,
Hath fashioned each manifold chord
To utter His visible Word,

Whose work, wheresoever begun,
Like the rays floating back to the Sun,
In the soul of all beauty is *one*.

TO THE SUMMER WIND.

ART thou the selfsame wind that blew
When I was but a boy?
Thy voice is like the voice I knew,
And yet the thrill of joy
Has softened to a sadder tone—
Perchance the echo of mine own.

Beside a sea of memories
In solitude I dwell:
Upon the shore forsaken lies
Alas! no murmuring shell!
Are all the voices lost to me
Still wandering the world with thee?

NARCISSUS.

THE god enamoured never knew
  The shadow that beguiled his view,
Nor deemed it less divinely true
  Than Life and Love.

And so the poet, while he wrought
His image in the tide of thought,
Deemed it a glimpse in darkness caught
  Of light above.

CHILDHOOD.

OLD Sorrow I shall meet again,
  And Joy, perchance — but never, never,
Happy Childhood, shall we twain
  See each other's face forever!

And yet I would not call thee back,
  Dear Childhood, lest the sight of me,
Thine old companion, on the rack
  Of Age, should sadden even thee.

TO AN OLD WASSAIL-CUP.

WHERE Youth and Laughter lingered long
To quaff delight, with wanton song
And warm caress,
Now Time and Silence strive amain
With lips unsatisfied, to drain
Life's emptiness!

FOUNTAIN-HEADS.

ALIKE from depths of joy and sorrow start
  The rain-drops of the heart:
Alike from sweet and briny waves arise
  The tear-drops of the skies.
And back to earth salt tears and freshening rain
  Alike must flow again.

THE REAPER.

TELL me whither, maiden June,
  Down the dusky slope of noon
With thy sickle of a moon,
  Goest thou to reap.

"Fields of Fancy by the stream
Of night in silvery silence gleam,
To heap with many a harvest-dream
  The granary of Sleep."

THE BUTTERFLY.

LEAFLESS, stemless, floating flower,
From a rainbow's scattered bower,
Like a bubble of the air
Blown by fairies, tell me where
Seed or scion I may find
Bearing blossoms of thy kind.

THE STRANGER.

HE ENTERED; but the mask he wore
   Concealed his face from me.
Still, something I had seen before
   He brought to memory.

"Who art thou? What thy rank, thy name?"
   I questioned, with surprise;
"*Thyself*," the laughing answer came,
   "*As seen of others' eyes.*"

JOY.

NEW-BORN, how long to stay?
The while a dew-drop may,
Or rainbow-gleam:
One kiss of sun or shade,
And, lo, the breath that made,
Unmakes the dream!

REGRET.

WHAT pleading passion of the dark
  Hath left the Morning pale?
She listens! "'T is, alas, the Lark,
  And not the Nightingale!
O for the gloom-encircled sphere,
  Whose solitary bird
Outpours for Love's awakening ear
  What noon hath never heard!"

SLEEP.

BLIND art thou as thy mother Night,
And as thy sister Silence dumb;
But naught of soothing sound or sight
Doth unto mortals come
So tender as thy fancied glance
And dream-imagined utterance.

YORICK'S SKULL.

POOR jester! still upon the stage,
  Chap-fallen flung,
Where merry clowns from age to age
  Thy dirge have sung;
Yet more than Eloquence may reach,
  Thought-heights among:
'T is thine, humanity to teach,
  Sans brains or tongue.

KEATS — SAPPHO.

METHINKS, when first the nightingale
Was mated to thy deathless song,
That Sappho with emotion pale,
Amid the Olympian throng,
Again, as in the Lesbian grove,
Stood listening with lips apart,
To hear in thy melodious love
The pantings of her heart.

THE BROOK.

IT is the mountain to the sea
That makes a messenger of me:
And, lest I loiter on the way
And lose what I am sent to say,
He sets his reverie to song
And bids me sing it all day long.
Farewell! for here the stream is slow,
And I have many a mile to go.

KILLDEE.

KILLDEE! Killdee! far o'er the lea
  At twilight comes the cry.
Killdee! a marsh-mate answereth
  Across the shallow sky.

Killdee! Killdee! thrills over me
  A rhapsody of light,
As star to star gives utterance
  Between the day and night.

Killdee! Killdee! O Memory,
  The twin birds, Joy and Pain,
Like shadows parted by the sun,
  At twilight meet again!

THE MOCKING-BIRD.

O HEART that cannot sleep for song!
  Behold, I wake with thee,
And drink, as from a fountain strong,
  Thy midnight melody,
That, poured upon the thirsting silence, seems
  Fresh from the shade of dreams

My spirit, like the sapless bough
  Of some long-wintered tree,
Feels suddenly the life that now
  Sets all thy passion free,
And flushed as in the wakening strength of wine,
  Leaps heavenward with thine.

THE HUMMING-BIRD.

A FLASH of harmless lightning,
  A mist of rainbow dyes,
The burnished sunbeams brightening,
  From flower to flower he flies:

While wakes the nodding blossom,
  But just too late to see
What lip hath touched her bosom
  And drained her nectary.

THE LARK.

HE rose, and singing passed from sight:—
  A shadow kindling with the sun,
His joy ecstatic flamed, till light
  And heavenly song were one.

THE BLUEBIRD.

'TIS thine the earliest song to sing
Of welcome to the wakening spring,
Who round thee, as a blossom, weaves
The fragrance of her sheltering leaves.

TO A WOOD-ROBIN.

LO, where the blooming woodland wakes
From wintry slumbers long,
Thy heart, a bud of silence, breaks
To ecstasy of song.

BLOSSOM.

FOR this the fruit, for this the seed,
 For this the parent tree;
The least to man, the most to God —
 A fragrant mystery
Where Love, with Beauty glorified,
Forgets Utility.

TO A ROSE.

THOU hast not toiled, sweet Rose,
  Yet needest rest;
Softly thy petals close
  Upon thy breast,
Like folded hands, of labor long oppressed.

Naught knowest thou of sin,
  Yet tears are thine;
Baptismal drops within
  Thy chalice shine,
At morning's birth, at evening's calm decline.

Alas! one day hath told
  The tale to thee!
Thy tender leaves enfold
  Life's mystery:
Its shadow falls alike on thee and me!

THE WATER-LILY.

WHENCE, O fragrant form of light,
Hast thou drifted through the night,
Swanlike, to a leafy nest,
On the restless waves, at rest?

Art thou from the snowy zone
Of a mountain-summit blown,
Or the blossoms of a dream,
Fashioned in the foamy stream?

Nay; methinks the maiden moon,
When the daylight came too soon,
Fleeting from her bath to hide,
Left her garment in the tide.

THE PLAINT OF THE ROSE.

SAID the budding Rose, "All night
Have I dreamed of the joyous light:
  How long doth my lord delay!
Come, Dawn, and kiss from mine eyes away
The dewdrops cold and the shadows gray,
  That hide thee from my sight!"

Said the full-blown Rose, "O Light!
(So fair to the dreamer's sight!)
  How long doth the dew delay!
Come back, sweet sister shadows gray,
And lead me home from the world away,
  To the calm of the cloister Night!"

THE VIOLET SPEAKS.

THINK not yon star,
New-found afar,
Love's latest sign;
Nor fondly dream
No fresher beam
Doth on thee shine:
A newer light,
From longer night
Of years, is mine.

TO THE VIOLET.

SWEET violet, who knows
From whence thy fragrance flows
Or whither hence it goes?

A pious pilgrim here
To Winter's sepulchre
Thou comest year by year

Alert with balmier store
Than Magdalen of yore
To Love's anointing bore.

Methinks that thou hast been
So oft the go-between
'Twixt sight and things unseen

That with thy wafted breath
Alternate echoeth
Each bank of sundering Death.

GOLDEN-ROD.

AS Israel, in days of old,
  Beneath the prophet's rod,
Amid the waters, backward rolled,
  A path triumphant trod;
So, while thy lifted staff appears,
  Her pilgrim steps to guide,
The Autumn journeys on, nor fears
  The Winter's threatening tide.

STAR-JESSAMINE.

DISCERNING Star from Sister Star,
We give to each its name;
But ye, O countless Blossoms, are
In fragrance and in flame
So like, that He from whom ye came
Alone discerneth each by name.

THE DANDELION.

WITH locks of gold to-day;
To-morrow, silver gray;
Then blossom-bald. Behold,
O man, thy fortune told!

FERN SONG.

DANCE to the beat of the rain, little Fern,
And spread out your palms again,
  And say, "Tho' the sun
  Hath my vesture spun,
He had labored, alas, in vain,
  But for the shade
  That the Cloud hath made,
And the gift of the Dew and the Rain."
  Then laugh and upturn
  All your fronds, little Fern,
And rejoice in the beat of the rain!

AUTUMN GOLD.

DEATH in the house, and the golden-rod
A-bloom in the field!
O blossom, how, from the lifeless clod,
When the fires are out and the ashes cold,
Doth a vein that the miners know not, yield
Such wealth of gold?

AUTUMN SONG.

MY life is but a leaf upon the tree —
A growth upon the stem that feedeth all.
A touch of frost — and suddenly I fall,
To follow where my sister-blossoms be.

The selfsame sun, the shadow, and the rain,
That brought the budding verdure to the bough,
Shall strip the fading foliage as now,
And leave the limb in nakedness again.

My life is but a leaf upon the tree;
The winds of birth and death upon it blow;
But whence it came and whither it shall go,
Is mystery of mysteries to me.

INDIAN SUMMER.

'TIS said, in death, upon the face
Of Age, a momentary trace
Of Infancy's returning grace
Forestalls decay;

And here, in Autumn's dusky reign,
A birth of blossom seems again
To flush the woodland's fading train
With dreams of May.

DECEMBER.

DULL sky above, dead leaves below;
And hungry winds that whining go.
Like faithful hounds upon the track
Of one beloved that comes not back.

AT THE YEAR'S END.

NIGHT dreams of day, and winter seems
In sleep to breathe the balm of May.
Their dreams are true anon; but they,
The dreamers, then, alas, are dreams.

Thus, while our days the dreams renew
Of some forgotten sleeper, we,
The dreamers of futurity,
Shall vanish when our own are true.

THE CHRISTMAS BABE.

SO *small* that lesser lowliness
Must bow to worship or caress;
So *great* that heaven itself to know
Love's majesty must look below.

THE LIGHT OF BETHLEHEM.

'Tis Christmas night! the snow,
  A flock unnumbered lies:
The old Judean stars aglow,
  Keep watch within the skies.

An icy stillness holds
  The pulses of the night:
A deeper mystery infolds
  The wondering Hosts of Light.

Till, lo, with reverence pale
  That dims each diadem,
The lordliest, earthward bending, hail
  The Light of Bethlehem!

OUT OF BOUNDS.

A LITTLE Boy of heavenly birth,
  But far from home to-day,
Comes down to find His ball, the Earth,
  That Sin has cast away.
O comrades, let us one and all
Join in to get Him back His ball!

MISTLETOE.

TO the cradle-bough of a naked tree,
Benumbed with ice and snow,
A Christmas dream brought suddenly
A birth of mistletoe.

The shepherd stars from their fleecy cloud
Strode out on the night to see;
The Herod north-wind blustered loud
To rend it from the tree.

But the old year took it for a sign,
And blessed it in his heart:
"With prophecy of peace divine,
Let now my soul depart."

EASTER.

LIKE a meteor, large and bright,
Fell a golden seed of light
On the field of Christmas night
  When the Babe was born;
Then 't was sepulchred in gloom
Till above His holy tomb
Flashed its everlasting bloom —
  Flower of Easter morn.

EASTER LILIES.

THOUGH long in wintry sleep ye lay,
The powers of darkness could not stay
Your coming at the call of day,
Proclaiming spring.

Nay; like the faithful virgins wise,
With lamps replenished ye arise,
Ere dawn the death anointed eyes
Of Christ, the king.

RESURRECTION.

ALL that springeth from the sod
Tendeth upwards unto God;
All that cometh from the skies
Urging it anon to rise.

Winter's life-delaying breath
Leaveneth the lump of death,
Till the frailest fettered bloom
Moves the earth, and bursts the tomb.

Welcome, then, Time's threshing-pain
And the furrows where each grain,
Like a Samson, blossom-shorn,
Waits the resurrection morn.

AWAKENING.

DO they that sleep, O Blossoms, yearn,
When ye from them to us return,
Again with you to rise?
Or do they in your quickening breath
Speak to us from the shades of death,
And see us with your eyes?

EARTH'S TRIBUTE.

FIRST the grain, and then the blade —
The one destroyed, the other made;
Then stalk and blossom, and again
The gold of newly minted grain.

So Life, by Death the reaper cast
To earth, again shall rise at last;
For 't is the service of the sod
To render God the things of God.

THE RECOMPENSE.

SHE brake the box, and all the house was filled
With waftures from the fragrant store thereof,
While at His feet a costlier vase distilled
The bruised balm of penitential love.

And, lo, as if in recompense of her,
Bewildered in the lingering shades of night,
He breaks anon the sealed sepulchre,
And fills the world with rapture and with light.

RABBONI!

"I BRING Thee balm, and, lo, Thou art not here!
Twice have I poured mine ointment on Thy brow,
And washed Thy feet with tears. Disdain'st Thou now
The spikenard and the myrrh?

Has Death, alas, betrayed Thee with a kiss
That seals Thee from the memory of mine?"
"Mary!" It is the self-same Voice Divine.
"Rabboni!"— only this.

TO THE CHRIST.

THOU hast on earth a Trinity, —
Thyself, my fellow-man, and me;
When one with him, then one with Thee;
Nor, save together, Thine are we.

THE IMMACULATE CONCEPTION.

A DEW-DROP of the darkness born,
  Wherein no shadow lies;
The blossom of a barren thorn,
  Whereof no petal dies;
A rainbow beauty passion-free,
Wherewith was veiled Divinity.

THE ANNUNCIATION.

"FIAT!"—The flaming word
Flashed, as the brooding Bird
Uttered the doom far heard
Of Death and Night.

"Fiat!"—A cloistered womb—
A sealed, untainted tomb—
Wakes to the birth and bloom
Of Life and Light.

THE INCARNATION.

SAVE through the flesh Thou wouldst not come
to me—
The flesh, wherein Thy strength my weakness found
A weight to bow Thy Godhead to the ground,
And lift to Heaven a lost humanity.

THE ASSUMPTION.

NOR Bethlehem nor Nazareth
Apart from Mary's care;
Nor heaven itself a home for Him
Were not His mother there.

MAGDALEN. (AFTER SWINBURNE.)

"SHE hath done what she could."
It was thus that He spake of her,
Trembling and pale as the penitent stood.
"And this she hath done shall be told for the sake of her,
Told as embalmed in the gift that I take of her,
Take, as an earnest of all that she would
Who hath done what she could.

"She hath done what she could:
Lo, the flame that hath driven her
Downward, is quenched! and her grief like a flood
In the strength of a rain-swollen torrent hath shriven her:
Much hath she loved and much is forgiven her;
Love in the longing fulfils what it would —
She hath done what she could."

ABSOLVED.

FAR floating o'er its native fen,
The evening Cloud, like Magdalen—
Her penitential tears
Assuaged of Love, her sins forgiven—
Upborne upon a waveless heaven
Of radiant rest, appears.

THE PRECURSOR.

"AS John of old before His face did go
To make the rough ways smooth, that all might know
The level road that leads to Bethlehem, lo,
I come," proclaims the snow.

SON OF MARY.

SHE the mother was of One —
Christ, her Saviour and her Son.
And another had she none?
Yea: her Love's beloved — **John.**

CHRIST TO THE VICTIM-TREE.

SOON, but not alone to die,
  Kinsman Tree,
Limbed and leafless must thou lie,
  Doomed, alas, for Me;
Yea, for Me, as I for all,
Must thou first a victim fall.

Thou for me the bitter fruit
  Loth to bear,
Must of Death's accursed root
  Shame reluctant share.
Thus the Father's will divine
Seals thy fate to compass Mine.

ANGELS OF PAIN.

AH, should they come revisiting the spot
Whence by our prayers we drove them utterly,
Shame were it for their saddened eyes to see
How soon their visitations are forgot.

A LENTEN THOUGHT.

ALONE with Thee, who canst not be alone,
  At midnight, in Thine everlasting day;
Lo, less than naught, of nothingness undone,
    I, prayerless, pray!

Behold — and with Thy bitterness make sweet,
  What sweetest is in bitterness to hide —
Like Magdalen, I grovel at Thy feet,
    In lowly pride.

Smite, till my wounds beneath Thy scourging cease;
  Soothe, till my heart in agony hath bled;
Nor rest my soul with enmity at peace,
    Till Death be dead.

"IS THY SERVANT A DOG?"

SO *must* he be who, in the crowded street,
Where shameless Sin and flaunting Pleasure meet,
Amid the noisome footprints finds the sweet
Faint vestige of Thy feet.

HOLY GROUND.

PAUSE where apart the fallen sparrow lies,
  And lightly tread;
For there the pity of a Father's eyes
  Enshrines the dead.

THE PLAYMATES.

WHO are thy playmates, boy ?
"My favorite is Joy,
Who brings with him his sister, Peace, to stay
The livelong day.
I love them both; but he
Is most to me."

And where thy playmates now,
O man of sober brow ?
"Alas! dear Joy, the merriest, is dead.
But I have wed
Peace; and our babe, a boy,
New-born, is Joy."

TO THE BABE NIVA.

NIVA, Child of Innocence,
Dust to dust *we* go:
Thou, when Winter wooed thee hence,
Wentest snow to snow.

A PHONOGRAPH.

HARK! what his fellow-warblers heard
And uttered in the light,
Their phonograph, the mocking-bird,
Repeats to them at night.

A CRADLE-SONG.

SING it, Mother! sing it low:
  Deem it not an idle lay.
In the heart 't will ebb and flow
  All the life-long way.

Sing it, Mother! softly sing,
  While he slumbers on thy knee;
All that after-years may bring
  Shall flow back to thee.

Sing it, Mother, Love is strong!
  When the tears of manhood fall,
Echoes of thy cradle-song
  Shall its peace recall.

Sing it, Mother! when his ear
  Catcheth first the Voice Divine,
Dying, he may smile to hear
  What he deemeth thine.

CONFIDED.

ANOTHER lamb, O Lamb of God, behold,
Within this quiet fold,
Among Thy Father's sheep
I lay to sleep!
A heart that never for a night did rest
Beyond its mother's breast.
Lord, keep it close to Thee,
Lest waking it should bleat and pine for me!

THE TAX-GATHERER.

"AND pray, who are you?"
Said the violet blue
To the Bee, with surprise
At his wonderful size,
In her eye-glass of dew.

"I, madam," quoth he,
"Am a publican Bee,
Collecting the tax
On honey and wax.
Have you nothing for me?"

BABY.

BABY in her slumber smiling,
Doth a captive take:
Whispers Love, "From dreams beguiling
May she never wake!"

When the lids, like mist retreating,
Flee the azure deep,
Wakes a newborn Joy, repeating,
"May she never sleep!"

BABY'S DIMPLES.

LOVE goes playing hide-and-seek
'Mid the roses on her cheek,
With a little imp of Laughter,
Who, the while he follows after,
Leaves the footprints that we trace
All about the Kissing-place.

A BUNCH OF ROSES.

THE rosy mouth and rosy toe
  Of little baby brother,
Until about a month ago
  Had never met each other;
But nowadays the neighbors sweet,
  In every sort of weather,
Half way with rosy fingers meet,
  To kiss and play together.

THE NEW-YEAR BABE.

TWO together, Babe and Year,
  At the midnight chime,
Through the darkness drifted here
  To the coast of Time.

Two together, Babe and Year,
  Over night and day
Crossed the desert Winter drear
  To the land of May.

On together, Babe and Year,
  Swift to Summer passed;
"Rest a moment, Brother dear,"
  Said the Babe at last.

"Nay, but onward;" answered Year,
  "We must farther go:
Through the Vale of Autumn sere
  To the Mount of Snow."

Toiling upward, Babe and Year
  Climbed the frozen height.
"We may rest together here,
  Brother Babe — Good-night!"

Then together Babe and Year
  Slept: but ere the dawn,
Vanishing, I know not where,
  Brother Year was *gone!*

MILTON.

SO fair thy vision that the night
Abided with thee, lest the light,
A flaming sword before thine eyes,
Had shut thee out from Paradise.

TO SHELLEY.

AT Shelley's birth,
The Lark, dawn-spirit, with an anthem loud
  Rose from the dusky earth
  To tell it to the Cloud,
That, like a flower night-folded in the gloom,
  Burst into morning bloom.

  At Shelley's death,
The Sea, that deemed him an immortal, saw
  A god's extinguished breath,
  And landward, as in awe,
Upbore him to the altar whence he came,
  And the rekindling flame.

SAPPHO.

A LIGHT upon the headland, flaming far,
  We see thee o'er the widening waves of time,
Impassioned as a palpitating star,
  Big with prophetic destiny sublime:
A momentary flash — a burst of song —
  Then silence, and a withering blank of pain.
We wait, alas! in tedious vigils long,
  The meteor-gleam that cometh not again!
Our eyes are heavy, and our visage wan:
  Our breath — a phantom of the darkness — glides
Ghostlike to swell the dismal caravan
  Of shadows, where thy lingering splendor hides,
Till, with our tears and ineffectual sighs,
  We quench the spark a smouldering hope supplies.

TO SIDNEY LANIER.

THE dewdrop holds the heaven above,
   Wherein a lark, unseen,
Outpours a rhapsody of love
   That fills the space between.

My heart a dewdrop is, and thou,
   Dawn-spirit, far away,
Fillest the void between us now
   With an immortal lay.

ON THE FORTHCOMING VOLUME OF SIDNEY LANIER'S POEMS.

SNOW! Snow! Snow!
Do thy worst, Winter, but know, but know
That, when the Spring cometh, a blossom shall blow
From the heart of the Poet that sleeps below,
And his name to the ends of the earth shall go,
In spite of the snow!

FATHER DAMIEN.

O GOD, the cleanest offering
Of tainted earth below,
Unblushing to thy feet we bring —
"*A leper white as snow!*"

THE SNOWDROP.

"A NUN of Winter's sisterhood,"
A Snowdrop in the garden stood
Alone amid the solitude
That round her lay.

No sister blossom there was seen;
No memory of what had been;
No promise of returning green,
Or scented spray:

But she alone was bold to bear
The banner of the Spring, and dare,
In Winter's stern despite, declare
A gentler sway.

So didst thou, Damien, when the glow
Of faith and hope was waning low,
For souls bewintered dare the snow,
And lead the way.

QUATRAINS.

"FOR THE RAIN IT RAINETH EVERY DAY."

AY, every day the rain doth fall,
And every day doth rise:
'T is thus the heavens incessant call,
And thus the earth replies.

THE MAST.

THE winds that once my playmates were
No more my voice responsive hear,
Nor know me, naked now and dumb,
When o'er my wandering way they come.

A STONE'S THROW.

LO, Death another pebble far doth fling
  Into the midmost sea,
To leave of Life an ever-widening ring
  Upon Eternity.

LOVE'S AUTOGRAPH.

ONCE only did he pass my way.
  "When wilt thou come again?
Ah, leave some token of thy stay!"
  He wrote (and vanished) "Pain."

RENEWAL.

EACH Hagar month beholds her waning moon
  Upon the desert night,
Like Ishmael, a famished wanderer, swoon
  From darkness into light.

PREJUDICE.

A LEAF may hide the largest star
  From Love's uplifted eye;
A mote of prejudice out-bar
  A world of Charity.

THE BUBBLE.

WHY should I stay? Nor seed nor fruit have I.
But, sprung at once to beauty's perfect round,
Nor loss, nor gain, nor change in me is found, —
A life-complete in death-complete to die.

O'ERSPENT.

MY soul is as a fainting noonday star,
  And thou, the absent night;
Haste, that thy healing shadow from afar
  May touch me into light.

IMAGINATION.

HERE Fancy far outdoes the deed;
So hath Eternity the need
Of telling more than Time has taught
To fill the boundaries of Thought.

RUIN.

A POWER beyond Perfection's dream is thine, —
A shadow that the dwindling shape outgrows
Of substance, like a vast horizon-line
Receding as the Fancy onward goes.

√

BECALMED.

THE bar is crossed: but Death — the pilot — stands
In seeming doubt before the tranquil deep;
The fathom-line still trembling in his hands,
As when upon the treacherous shoals of sleep.

TO THE SPHINX.

AH, not alone in Egypt's desert land
Thy dwelling-place apart!
But wheresoe'er the scorching passion-sand
Hath seared the human heart.

DISCREPANCY.

ONE dream the bird and blossom dreamed
Of Love, the whole night long;
Yet twain its revelation seemed,
  In fragrance and in song.

POETRY.

A GLEAM of heaven; the passion of a Star
Held captive in the clasp of harmony:
A silence, shell-like breathing from afar
The rapture of the deep,— eternity.

SAP.

STRONG as the sea, and silent as the grave,
  It ebbs and flows unseen;
Flooding the earth — a fragrant tidal wave —
  With mist of deepening green.

SLEEP.

WHAT art thou, balmy sleep?
"Foam from the fragrant deep
Of silence, hither blown
From the hushed waves of tone."

THE PYRAMIDS.

AMID the desert of a mystic land,
Like Sibyls waiting for a doom far-seen,
Apart in awful solitude they stand,
  With Thought's unending caravan between.

FORMATION.

WHATE'ER we love becomes of us a part;
  The centre of all tributary powers—
Our life is fed from Nature's throbbing heart,
  And of her best the fibred growth is ours.

THE PROMONTORY.

NOT all the range of sea-born liberty
  Hath ever for one restless wave sufficed:
So pants the heart, — of all compulsion free, —
  Self-driven to the Rock, its barrier, Christ.

STARS.

BEHOLD, upon the field of Night,
Far-scattered seeds of golden light;
Nor one to wither, but anon
To bear the heaven-full harvest, Dawn.

WHISPER.

CLOSE cleaving unto Silence, into sound
She ventures as a timorous child from land,
Still glancing, at each wary step, around,
  Lest suddenly she lose her sister's hand.

THE SUN.

HE prisons many a life indeed
Within the narrow cells of seed,
But cannot call them forth again
Without the sesame of rain.

THE SUNBEAM.

A LADDER from the Land of Light,
  I rest upon the sod,
Whence dewy angels of the Night
  Climb back again to God.

ALTER EGO.

THOU art to me as is the sea
  Unto the shell;
A life whereof I breathe, a love
  Wherein I dwell.

REFLECTION.

LIKE stars that in the waves below
With heaven's reflected splendor glow,
The flowers, in all their glory bright,
Are shadows of a fairer light.

ESTRANGEMENT.

WHAT kindly Absence hid, forsooth,
  Thy Presence late hath shown;
That, like a garment worn in youth,
I am, alas, outgrown!

BEETHOVEN AND ANGELO.

ONE made the surging sea of tone
  Subservient to his rod:
One, from the sterile womb of stone,
  Raised children unto God.

THE SHADOW.

O SHADOW, in thy fleeting form I see
The friend of fortune that once clung to me.
In flattering light, thy constancy is shown;
In darkness, thou wilt leave me all alone.

SONNETS.

THE INDIAN OF SAN SALVADOR.

WHAT time the countless arrow-heads of light
Keen twinkled on the bended heavens, back-drawn
With deadly aim, at signal of the Dawn,
To slay the slumbering, dusky warrior, Night;
I dreamed a dream: And, lo! three spirits, white
As mist that gathers when the rain is gone,
Came walking o'er the waters, whereupon
The very waves seemed quivering with affright.
I woke and heard, while yet the vision stayed,
A prophecy: "Behold the coming race
Before whose feet the forest kings shall fall
Prostrate; and ye, like twilight shadows tall
That wither at the sun's uplifted face,
Shall pass in silence to a deeper shade."

KEATS.

UPON thy tomb 't is graven, "Here lies one
Whose name is writ in water." Could there be
A flight of Fancy fitlier feigned for thee,
A fairer motto for her favorite son?
For, as the wave, thy varying numbers run —
Now crested proud in tidal majesty,
Now tranquil as the twilight reverie
Of some dim lake the white moon looks upon

While teems the world with silence. Even there,
In each Protean rainbow-tint that stains
The breathing canvas of the atmosphere,
We read an exhalation of thy strains.
Thus, on the scroll of Nature, everywhere,
Thy name, a deathless syllable, remains.

SILENCE.

TEMPLE of God, from all eternity
  Alone like Him without beginning found;
  Of time and space and solitude the bound,
Yet in thyself of all communion free.
Is, then, the temple holier than He
  That dwells therein? Must reverence surround
  With barriers the portal, lest a sound
Profane it? Nay; behold a mystery!

What was, abides; what is, hath ever been:
  The lowliest the loftiest sustains.
A silence, by no breath of utterance stirred —
  Virginity in motherhood — remains,
Clear, midst a cloud of all-pervading sin,
  The voice of Love's unutterable word.

UNUTTERED.

WAITING for words — as on the broad expanse
  Of heaven the formless vapors of the night,
  Expectant, wait the oracle of light
Interpreting their dumb significance;
Or like a star that in the morning glance
  Shrinks, like a folding blossom, from the sight,
  Nor wakens till upon the western height
The shadows to their evening towers advance —

So, in my soul, a dream ineffable,
  Expectant of the sunshine or the shade,
Hath oft, upon the brink of twilight chill,
  Or at the dawn's pale glimmering portal stayed
In tears, that all the quivering eyelids fill,
  In smiles, that on the lip of silence fade.

SOLITUDE.

THOU wast to me what to the changing year
Its seasons are, — a joy forever new;
What to the night its stars, its heavenly dew,
Its silence; what to dawn its lark-song clear;
To noon, its light — its fleckless atmosphere,
Where ocean and the overbending blue,
In passionate communion, hue for hue,
As one in Love's circumference appear.

O brimming heart, with tears for utterance
Alike of joy and sorrow! lift thine eyes
And sphere the desolation. Love is flown;
And in the desert's widening expanse
Grim Silence, like a sepulchre of stone,
Stands charnelling a soul's funereal sighs.

LOVE'S RETROSPECT.

I KNEW that he was dying; for the leaves
  Late-fallen, shivered on the frosty ground,
  Disconsolate, with the foreboding sound
That Autumn whispers to the hearts that grieves.
The sunshine, slanting upward, smote the sheaves
  O'ershadowing the hill-tops ranged around,
  And where the swallow's empty nest was found,
  Spattered, as if with blood, the sheltering eves.

Twin fires together faded: and but one
  Rewakened o'er a world henceforth to me
  In evetlasting twilight. To the Past
The Present pays its tribute, whereupon
  Each moment coins the selfsame effigy, —
  The more than all by wealth unwidowed cast.

A WINTER TWILIGHT.

BLOOD-SHOTTEN through the bleak gigantic trees
The sunset, o'er a wilderness of snow,
Startles the wolfish winds that wilder grow
As hunger mocks their howling miseries.
In every skulking shadow Fancy sees
The menace of an undiscovered foe —
A sullen footstep, treacherous and slow,
That comes, or into deeper darkness flees.

Nor Day nor Night, in Time's eternal round
Whereof the tides are telling, e'er hath passed
This Isthmus-hour — this dim, mysterious land
That sets their lives asunder — where up-cast
Their earliest and their latest waves resound,
As each, alternate, nears or leaves the strand.

GLIMPSES.

AS one who in the hush of twilight hears
The pausing pulse of Nature, when the Light
  Commingles in the dim mysterious rite
Of Darkness with the mutual pledge of tears,
Till soft, anon, one timorous star appears,
  Pale-budding as the earliest blossom white
  That comes in Winter's livery bedight,
To hide the gifts of genial Spring she bears, —

So, unto me — what time the mysteries
  Of consciousness and slumber weave a dream
    And pause above it with abated breath,
Like intervals in music — lights arise,
  Beyond prophetic Nature's farthest gleam,
    That teach me half the mystery of Death.

THE AGONY.

I WRESTLED, as did Jacob, till the dawn,
With the reluctant Spirit of the Night
That keeps the keys of Slumber. Worn and white,
We paused a panting moment, while anon
The darkness paled around us. Thereupon —
His mighty limbs relaxing in affright —
The Angel pleaded: "Lo, the morning light!
O Israel, release me, and begone!"

Then said I, "Nay, a captive to my will
I hold thee till the blessing thou dost keep
Be mine." Whereat he breathed upon my brow;
And, as the dew upon the twilight hill,
So on my spirit, over-wearied now,
Came tenderly the benediction, Sleep.

THE DEAD TREE.

ERECT in death thou standest gaunt and bare,
Thy limbs uplifted to the wintry sky,
To supplicate its pity, or defy
The threat of wrath with towering despair.
Around thee, like a wizard's widening snare,
Lithe shadows in a web fantastic lie,
Spun of the moon, in midnight sorcery,
Down gazing with a madman's vacant stare.

What reads she in thy ruin? Lives the past
Recorded in the present? Lingers here
The legend of a glory overcast,
The song of birds long silent, and the stir
Of leaves forever scattered to the blast,
Yet echoed in eternal dreams to her?

HOMELESS.

METHINKS that if my spirit could behold
Its earthly habitation void and chill,
  Whence all its time-encircled good and ill
Expanded to eternity, 't would fold
Its trembling pinions o'er the bosom cold,
  Recalling there the pulse's wonted thrill,
  And lean, perchance, to catch the echo still
That erst in life the dream of passion told.

How calm the dissolution! Could she spurn
  Her spouse, so late, and brother? Could she trace
The strange familiar lineaments, and mark
  The doom of her own writing in the face,
To find, alas! no more the vital spark,
  Nor breathe one sigh of pity to return?

THE PETREL.

A WANDERER o'er the sea-graves ever green,
Whereon the foam-flowers blossom day by day,
Thou flittest as a doomful shadow gray
That from the wave no sundering light can wean.
What wouldst thou from the deep unfathomed glean,
Frail voyager? and whither leads thy way?
Or art thou, as the sailor legends say,
An exile from the spirit-world unseen?

Lo! desolate, above a colder tide,
Pale Memory, a sea-bird like to thee,
Flits outward where the whitening billows hide
What seemed of Life the one reality, —
A mist whereon the morning bloom hath died,
Returning, ghost-like, to the restless sea.

AT ANCHOR.

HOW calm upon the twilight water sleeps,
With folded wings, yon solitary sail,
Safe-harbored, haply dreaming of the gale
That wolf-like o'er the waste deserted leaps:
One star — a signal light above her — keeps
Watch; and, behold, its pictured image pale
Gleams far below, a seeming anchor frail,
Where onward still the noiseless current sweeps.

Star of my life, pale planet, far removed,
Oh, be thou, when the twilight deepens, near!
Set in my soul thine image undisproved
By death and darkness, till the morning clear
Behold me in the presence I have loved,
My beacon here, my bliss eternal there!

SHADOWS.

YE shrink not wholly from us when the morn
Arises red with slaughter, and the slain
Sweet visages of tender dreams remain
To haunt us through the wakened hours forlorn,
Nor when the noontide cometh, and the thorn
Of light is centred in the quivering brain,
And Memory her pilgrimage of pain
Renews, with fainting footsteps, overworn.

Nay, then, what time the satellite of day
Pursues his path victorious, and the West,
Her clouds beleaguered vanishing away,
A desert seems of solitude oppressed,
Around us still your hovering pinions stay,
The pledges of returning night and rest.

THE MOUNTAIN.

ALTAR whereon the lordly sacrifice
Of incense from the reverent vales below
  Is offered at the dawn's first kindling glow
And when the day's last smouldering ember dies,
Around thee, too, the kindred sympathies
  Of life — itself a vapor — breathe and flow,
  And yearn beyond thy pinnacle of snow
To wing the trackless region of the skies.

Thy shadow broods above me, and mine own
  Sleeps as a child beneath it. O'er my dreams
    Thou dost, as an abiding presence, pour
Thy spirit in the melancholy moan
  Of cavern winds and far-resounding streams,
    As sings the ocean to the listening shore.

UNMOORED.

TO die in sleep — to drift from dream to dream
Along the banks of slumber, beckoned on
Perchance by forms familiar, till anon,
Unconsciously, the ever-widening stream
Beyond the breakers bore thee, and the beam
Of everlasting morning woke upon
Thy dazzled gaze, revealing one by one
Thy visions grown immortal in its gleam.

O blessed consummation! thus to feel
In Death no touch of terror. Tenderly
As shadows to the evening hills, he came
In garb of God's dear messenger to thee,
Nor on thy weary eyelids broke the seal,
In reverence for a brother's holier name.

EUGENIE.

IN exile, widowed, childless, desolate,
Thou sittest in the majesty of woe ;
And nations gaze, with shuddering murmurs low,
Upon the direful trilogy of Fate.
Hushed are the warring interests of state
Beneath the pall of Sorrow. Foes forego
Their wonted discord, and with footsteps slow
And meekened foreheads, move compassionate.

All exiles weave their miseries with thine;
All widows turn with sympathy to thee;
All mothers desolate and childless made,
Mingle their moan with this thine agony:
And yet, to thee the royal lot is laid —
Threefold the cross that measures love divine.

THE PASCHAL MOON.

THY face is whitened with remembered woe;
  For thou alone, pale satellite, didst see,
  Amid the shadows of Gethsemane,
The mingled cup of sacrifice o'erflow;
Nor hadst the power of utterance to show
  The wasting wound of silent sympathy,
  Till sudden tides, obedient to thee,
Sobbed, desolate in weltering anguish, low.

The holy night returneth year by year;
  And, while the mystic vapors from thy rim
Distil the dews, as from the Victim there
  The red drops trickled in the twilight dim,
The ocean's changeless threnody we hear,
  And gaze upon thee as thou didst on Him.

GOLGOTHA.

ALONE I stand upon the sacred height,
  Where erst, at noon, the night its mantle flung
  O'er the Divine Humanity that hung
To brutal gaze exposed. The conscious light
To sudden blindness withered at the sight
  Of mortal pangs from wounds immortal wrung;
  The earth her gates sepulchral open swung,
Impatient for the soul's descending flight

To her expectant shades. O Calvary!
  Again the dripping darkness crowns thy brow,
    And I (as then, to His all-seeing mind)
Weep 'mid the general gloom. Oh! let me be,
  As in those hours of anguish, hidden now
    In shades of death, the light of life to find.

THE PORTRAIT.

EACH has his Angel-Guardian. Mine, I know,
Looks on me from that pictured face. Behold,
How clear, between those rifted clouds of gold,
The radiant brow! It is the morning glow
Of Innocence, ere yet the heart let go
The leading-strings of Heaven. Upon the eyes
No shadow: like the restful noonday skies
They sanctify the teeming world below.

Why bows my soul before it? None but thou,
O tender child, has known the life estranged
From thee and all that made thy days of joy
The measure of my own. Behold me now —
The man that begs a blessing of the boy —
His very *self;* but from himself how changed!

THIS FIRST EDITION OF POEMS BY JOHN B. TABB IS LIMITED TO FIVE HUNDRED COPIES, WHICH HAVE BEEN PRINTED DURING THE AUTUMN OF 1894 BY JOHN WILSON AND SON, CAMBRIDGE, MASSACHUSETTS.

www.ingramcontent.com/pod-product-compliance
Lightning Source LLC
LaVergne TN
LVHW011228110826
845150LV00006B/1577

9781425514952